The Girl I Was: Selfie Queen

Lisa Douglass

ISBN: **9781981057733**
ISBN-13:

DEDICATION

I dedicate this book to my mother and my father who
Gave me my beautiful face and taught
Me almost everything I know; I dedicate this book to the men
and women, my friends who lost their faces due to USC's
targeting of rhinoplasty patients who used deceit and stole our
faces; and I dedicate this book to God, and the doctors and
lawyers who helped me.

CONTENTS

This is a photo essay about my life before.

ACKNOWLEDGMENTS

I acknowledge my writing mentors: Mona Simpson and Les Plesko.
And Dollface, who helped me find the mysteries of what happened to me. To the wonderful Doctor Ion who is still trying to get me back to my old self.

1 THE SELFIE

When I discovered selfies.
I discovered myself.
I'm what is considered an insanely shy artist.
An extrovert behind the screen.
IRL a silent observer.

I felt it was a way to empower my individual identity. Make myself feel confident by just being my authentic self.

That's me halfway up the ladder
That's me in the mirror
That's me wherever you left me
Standing holding my water bottle.
I was worried, I told everyone about it
My life going on like a concerto
I was not what you wanted me to be.
I was a terrible failure at life.
But I had my beauty
And my brain.
That's me on the table
Students standing over me
Deciding what to destroy first.
That's me in the hallway, I see me running out
The nurse chased me and didn't let me leave
This time I made it
And I wouldn't know each of you

Because I would still be me.

Things they stole from us. Dating. Selfies.
Happiness. Human Emotion. Sleep. Sex. Beauty.
Uniqueness. Our wonderful lives.

And in pictures I always looked
two ways: confident and
exactly like I wanted to look.

Each image was a statement
a who, a what, a where and
exactly how I was feeling.

LISA DOUGLASS

The Boyfriend

I'm not so much looking into his eyes anymore
Not like I should be
There is a disconnect, a counting
Almost as if I am a sacred thing that can
No longer speak
The boyfriend speaks infrequently
Brown hair matted like that
He wants connection and love, but I can't feel anything
But sad
I want to embrace him but I tell him to find a different
less broken girl
Someone with less fire.
He tried all that
It didn't work, he tells me
He sends a photo of the girl with tight leggings
She looks dumb.

like from a trailer

I made writing that went with the images. I didn't have to try to compete with the Kardashians because I had never been that kind of style-seeker. I have always loved photography and found the soul of the image to be in the eyes.

We were at Bergamot Station. I was thinking I could like him but he was like everyone else and tried to get me to have sex with him later that night. When I say "get me to," I mean he used all kinds of manipulation and I just told him I wasn't going to have sex with anyone who acted that way. He apologized later, but to my friends who ask me why I'm not seeing anyone, there are a string of men I have tried to see. But, when I break up they stalk me and if I go to the police, they do nothing. After what happened to me, I no longer feel safe in the world.

I had suffered abuse in childhood and found it difficult when someone was pushy.

. When I had diaries when I was younger, my mother read
them with my sister. They wanted to know my inner thoughts
but I had stopped speaking to them. My sister was abusing me
and my diary was my safe place.

I had been in AA many years and I found that the men there were sometimes unstable. That is not to say I don't love men. You will see some of them in this book. Boyfriends and other people I loved.

My friend Del had a television show and asked me to host. We interviewed a few different people and it was really fun. I have always loved being in front of the camera and never turned it down any opportunity to do that.

Like many actors, I worked for free a lot.

The way the world always tries to take from you and not give you anything, has always made me sad. I made money at writing though. I won a big award for a book I wrote at UCLA but by the time I figured out how to get an agent, she never sold it.

People had always told me I was special, and beautiful and brilliant, but I had things to overcome in myself. Sad things that had happened to me in childhood.

LISA DOUGLASS

In that Empty Room

It was a high-school gymnasium, basketball hoops on either
side, bleachers with the outlines of invisible teenagers--
dashes like on coupons cut from the newspaper---two giant
slicers rolled diagonally. The game was to run across and
not to die. I did that. Later, up on a giant sidewalk floating in
space, none of the concrete pieces touching, Lucille Ball
chased me and tried to pull me off. There was no bunny
rabbit. There was no neighborhood scare dog. There was no
prank call to the McDonald's strawberry shake. It was just
us. You weren't there. Don't keep saying you were.

You'll see in these photos, I change my furniture a lot. My style changes, but I always wear a little leather strand on my wrist and a silver and turquoise bracelet, if I can find it. I used to dress up everyday. But, my style is not committal edgy chic. Not so much polish, but attitude.

I got into a good grad school for writing after UCLA supported my writing as a fresh new voice. I won so many awards at UCLA that I stopped counting. I felt so happy and accomplished because my thoughts were seen as important and vital.

The one thing about me, is I have always felt relevant even after what happened to me. I saw a few photos yesterday of the actual thing, and I want to be honest here, I don't know how I survived it.

This photo exemplifies my
issues with men. I am looking

away and trying to be quiet.
There is a lurker in the
background, I don't know his
name and he will never know
me. Even my boyfriends never
seem to know me. I want them
to, but there are things
unreachable to friends and to
lovers.

This is my friend Peter
Rotsten. He is a wonderful
person and a unique one. Like
many unique people, I think he
gets misunderstood a lot. I
relate to him that way. He has a

brilliant mind though. We were at the Last Bookstore for some reading. I think it may have been Jerry Stahl's new book or it might have been my friend Jonathan Shaw's reading of his new book, Scab Vendor.

Here I was getting ready to go

to Nick Cave with my friend
Mike.
The main thing to remember
about this story is that I was in
life, out there every day, with
my friends.

This is Mike Coulter. He was in a very cool band, Lifter in the 1990's and has one of the best voices I've ever heard. He, like me, tries relationships more than stays in them.

This is one of my first
drawings. I wanted to see if I
could draw something beautiful
and I copied a magazine model.

It doesn't look like the model at all and I can't even remember which model it was, but it is beautiful anyway. It's a thing I made that shocks me every time I see it, because I think it's pretty good for not really having any talent in drawing.

This one was taken at the Ford Theater. We went to see Peaches. My friend on the left died of a heroin overdose a few months later. The other two I haven't seen since the tragedy when I disappeared from my own life.

This is my friend Christian
Stone. I have a lot to say about
Christian and how I feel about

him. I have so much respect for him but he is very good looking and it was always hard for me to be his friend because I would get uncomfortable by his looks and self-composure. One time I got invited to a game at his house and he was dating a girl I really admire. The game was Wolves and Villagers. And many of my friends had been invited for years and I never was. I always wanted to know what the game was and felt left out. The one time I got invited, I played to win and his girlfriend got mad at me and I was never invited again. Sometimes I think this is my exact experience in AA. I have tried to be friends with people without really knowing how. Was I supposed to play differently? It was the first time I'd ever been there. People see me one way but I'm insanely shy in lots of ways no one fathoms. I admire Christian and I wish life was different where you can be friends with people who either don't get you, don't like you or who make you uncomfortable for their beauty. I know I make people uncomfortable too at times. Even after everything.

I'm pretty sure this was still the

different outfits for Nick Cave
I was trying on. When
someone steals your face, your
whole life unravels. Mine got
stolen along with all that was
good about me. My vitality was
altered, my purity, my belief in
goodness. The ways I could be
brilliant changed because I
could no longer make
expressions that went with my
thoughts.

I gave away this jacket to the
homeless girls underneath the
bridge near my house. I wasn't

expecting to find girls down there, only guys living in tents and I wanted them to be warm because it was freezing in Los Angeles. When I got there with my friend Christian, there was a girl, a pretty black girl, who was obviously far from her home. I asked her if she could use the jacket and she thanked me. I remember thinking, she is too pretty to live with these guys under the bridge, but in way, she seemed very self composed and like she would be okay. I left feeling they would look out for her and that she had escaped something

beyond my comprehension. Something darker than living under that bridge.

When you are beautiful, you still get hurt by life a lot.
I had a man in AA tell me I was really ugly and a girl who
always had a parrot on her shoulder, wrote to me to tell me
she hated my selfies and they made her so angry. She told
me that I shouldn't seek validation for my face because she
really liked my writing. I always was amazed at how cruel
people could be. Here I was doing what everyone else in the
world was doing and getting hate for it, by someone in AA. I
never really understood that side of people. I always
celebrated people's beauty. I remember asking her about my
friend Neva who always photographed her body and this
woman told me she was a model and gets paid for it. The
dismissiveness of the human spirit still shocks me. Why
should my happiness or love of photography be hated. I
knew I didn't deserve it. I never went to her page to tell her

her parrot was stupid.

We don't always know how
others see us because they
never tell you. They might

think many many things about you but just never say it. In one way, I have become a voice for people without a voice. A face for people without a chance of getting well. I have tried my best to help people. But, every day I'm alive still, I miss my old life. I miss my face. I'm sad it happened.

The statistics that speak of
ghost surgeries, never include
the victims, because we aren't

supposed to know. It's a deception the educational institutions have used for decades. People won't know the difference and it helps medicine by teaching students on unsuspecting victims. But, I was a victim and I wasn't at a training hospital. USC students tried out cleft lip repairs on my beautiful face, when I just went in for something very very minor---a repair on the top of my bridge. I woke up and all my muscles of facial expression had been altered. I was a happy, confident person, I thought I had been very careful, but the doctor I saw, along with USC targets rhinoplasty patients in outside clinics to get students accredited by using private paying patients as human guinea pigs.

I didn't know the facts. Or the
regulatory laws that California
enacted that allow it to happen.

My doctor had an ad on his
website that promised no

human expression would be altered by such a minor procedure. But, like a serial killer won't tell you they are going to kill you, Dr. Andrew Frankel of Lasky Clinic has no conscience in destroying a person's life. Neither does USC. When I approached the board of medicine about it, The President Dr. **GnanaDev** told me he closes my complaints because the students are licensed. When I wrote to Michael Quick, the dean at USC Keck, he ignored me.

If something goes wrong, you
could sue, but no lawyer can
afford to take the case, so you

will be alone in the lawsuit
without your face. Or without
what makes you you to begin
with.

Ethicon's sutures, Vicryl went
from Class III, to Class II and
they even fought class II
against the US Government.
Class III, says it causes
unnecessary risk to the patient.
We all had those sutures in
each one of our op reports and
Dr. Frankel tells the students
to cut the cheek and then
suture it to a lower position
with a dissolvable cinch suture.
He knows how harmful that

can be because you can no
longer lift your mouth for
brushing your teeth or eating.
It made everything harder. But,
I didn't have the money to go
after Ethicon, who is owned by
Johnson and Johnson.

Dr. Frankel and Sim Choroomi
and Christian Paquet published
a paper in Jama about a Rim
Lowering procedure, but they
falsified the evidence. They cut
our cheeks and sutured our
noses to a lower position. LLC
repositioning wasn't the half of
it.

Not being able to smile is a cruelty that I never knew existed. I used to get bullied for my beauty. I never understood why men and women would reach out to me and tell me to quit seeking validation. I wasn't. I felt pretty and confident. I like photography and selfies were just one more means of artistic expression. I hate assumptions people have always made about why I do things, when I really just do things to be creative. I was accused once on Facebook of emotionally manipulating people because I did this video of me speaking in a southern accent. It was just an acting exercise. My friend Mike in AA

used to say people are extra
hard on me, and for reasons
unknowable, It's very true.

When you get hurt by a doctor,
all the other doctors refuse to
tell you what happened in case

you sue. So literally, your life is now one giant mystery of what happened to you and how to fix it. But, when you max out all your credit cards and you have to drive for Uber every day just to keep up with the finance fees, you will understand the burden is like being dead. Not being able to see your friends, is like being dead. Not being pretty anymore, or able to smile, is like being a prisoner of your own face. That someone did it deliberately to you, and no law enforcement agency will help you, shows state interest in

harming patients.

There are monsters in the

world. I had been too lucky and always been protected, but this time, the monster got me and killed my hopes and dreams and hoped I would not be like the phoenix to rise again. He told the students to cut so many muscles in my face, that I believe they hoped I would kill myself. I told him I was an actress and was so excited because I had just worked on State of Affairs. Alfre Woodard came up to me and told me I was so beautiful.

Dr. Frankel stole my life.

LISA DOUGLASS

So, did USC.
And the State of California did nothing about it.

In Nazi Germany, prisoners were experimented on without consent. They had no choice. Rules were set in place, to protect future patients called the Nuremberg Act that forbids Human Experimentation without an Experimental Bill of Rights but then the ACGME (The accreditation board to get licensed) mandated that 6 live rhinoplasty cases be conducted before a student gets accredited. I think it was only on cadavers before that. So, if they lure one patient, they "make the most" of the case. I had 26-46 un-consented to procedures done to my face. Most of them for cleft lip repair.

Looking back on what my life was like before is hard to do, but I try to remember it as I fight my way out of this hell. I had so many friends and such a good life. It's incomprehensible to me that California and America allows this to happen.

On the morning of surgery, Dr.
Frankel was acting off. Mean-
spirited, or on something on
something as a few others

friends recounted later. I tried to run out and tried to cancel. My boyfriend told me that Dr. Frankel had met with me four times and he knew what I wanted, but I didn't feel safe. Dr. Frankel tried to assure me again, anything could easily be fixed and promised to not remove any tissue. Told me again that I could easily be fixed by a revision in case I didn't love it. I told the nurse I was scared and didn't want to have surgery that day. The nurse told me Dr. Frankel was famous and a very good doctor, these comments were intended to get me to stay because they were using me as a test. Later I found this out. But, they gave me something and I couldn't run out, I passed out saying I was scared and didn't want to go through with surgery.

Later, after my entire face changed, Dr. Frankel told me I got old. He told me he could "try" to help me. He told me he regretted it. He had conned me, even up to the day, I'm pretty sure he was high and saw me laughing and pretty, right before my entire life was over.

Later, when I asked what happened to my footplates, because another doctor in town was so shocked someone cut them off.
He had Christian Paquet, also of USC Keck film Dr. Frankel cutting off footplates in a patient in his cell phone to show me it was tissue he didn't really need.

We all knew by then that the footplates contained the mouth muscles. But, when he did it to the patient on the morning of

September 20, 2016, I
recognized it. He disfigured
someone permanently forever
and ever to prove to me it was
tissue I really didn't

need.

This is me on the set of State of Affairs. We were in some downtown hotel. Maybe the

Biltmore.

My friend told me that she admired me because I
didn't try to hide my beauty. But, the truth was I
just liked my looks more than understood what
being beautiful meant. Being beautiful has to do

with your spirit. It has to do with compassion in your heart. But, I had a good face too. Being beautiful is not a curse. It's a gift. My beauty went with my mind and my thoughts and my heart. You have a thought, you make an expression, I can no longer make an expression. That doesn't look like a grimace. Smiling is the only thing that separates us from Monkeys. They Grimace. We smile. Here is one of the last photos where you can see my cheekbones, They cut out a giant square of my cheeks during what was meant to be a minor cosmetic procedure to add to the bridge of my nose and sutured it downward and inward to lower my eyes and nose, My cheeks can't lift anymore. They did this with Ethicon's sutures and left it off the reports.

When we asked what happened, he laughed at us, told us we were old, or held his nose up in the air like a pig and said, "I've never reversed it, you might look like a pig."

But the legal system isn't geared to help people, it's only geared to protect big business.

Just because lawyers turned me down, doesn't mean it wasn't the right thing to do suing. OJ Simpson walked away from murder but the Goldman's won against him in the Civil Case. The law doesn't side with victims; they just want you to give up. The judge thinks I'm still pretty somewhat. He just never saw what happened to me and I think he knows self-determination of the body is one of our god-given rights that was not honored.

Here I am with my friend on the set of some Television show. I can't remember what it was. But, they liked watching us walk around and kept telling everyone to look at us. My friend Dom is a model.

I had always wanted to be a model but I didn't know how. Lots of things I wanted to be, I didn't know how. The world is filled with rejection. I remember when I was an actress, getting headshots and thinking I couldn't get work because I wasn't a model. I remember not knowing how I looked to others. My boyfriends were always stalking me. I had a hard romantic life. Men I loved had issues I couldn't fix for them. I broke up a lot. I had told Dr. Frankel I was going back to acting. After seeing his consent form that he would re-do the procedure after a year for 25 percent off, I told him that that looked like he intended to mess it up. He lied and told me it was just for neurotic people. No one had come forward yet. I didn't know the hush agreements or the # Medical Board

took down his previous malpractice so he could target cosmetic patients for use as human guinea pigs in his outside clinic. I met with him three times to remove the filler in my nose. He knew exactly what I wanted.

Someone reached out to me on RealSelf and warned me about Dr. Frankel, and I stupidly asked Dr. Frankel and Vicky Diamond about it. I told them the woman or man told me that Dr. Frankel would do the opposite procedure and refuse to tell me what he had done. They assured me many neurotic people were on Realself. And he would never do that. I told them I wasn't like their ordinary patients and didn't have any more money to be fixed.

I still believe that they convinced me and used all kinds of methods to con me and were intentionally violent to my face because they knew I used all the money in the world and I told him I was going back to acting. Meanwhile, of course, I couldn't go back. My life was broken completely.

Adam Robinson from LaFollette Johnson stalked me online to find that I did a film for my friend, I was so embarrassed by my looks and it totally hurt our friendship. I explained it in a million ways, but Adam Robinson also told me that Human Experimentation was like an English Research paper. Human Research was like an English Research paper. He said on the record.

I had tried to make a few videos because it was a huge part of my life. I didn't look good anymore but I had tried just to stay alive and make art. Adam Robinson and the system was now going to use my efforts to try to stay alive against me. I'm sure they will show the jury that I did a film, that I thought was just for my friend. I didn't know he would submit it to 500 festivals. When he used me with all my muscles in my face cut

75

in a promotional material, I sobbed and begged him to take it down. To Adam Robinson, of LaFollette Johnson, this indicated that I was acting.

He did the thing I had been warned about. With malicious intent to destroy a life.

When my friend Kelly got pregnant. She was so scared. I
promised her that the money would come and she would
be able to take care of the twins. She called me crying a lot.
I knew that if she had Dylan and Emmy, she would be fine. I
trust the universe that these babies will always be cared for.

When I first started writing, I was surprised that anyone paid attention. People told me that my bravery was what always inspired them. I didn't feel brave, I just felt like telling my story and overcoming whatever fears I had about doing that.

I'd be a liar if I said I didn't think about dying. I thought about it a lot. I didn't do it only because I kept alive the hope that I could get better and we would find out what happened and maybe get fixed and be happy again. I never told my mother until last week and I didn't for many reasons but she told me she was so sorry it happened. I just couldn't tell her, it was too hard to do without crying. I'm crying now writing this, I never took my beauty or uniqueness for granted and the elective surgery world and laws try to make the assumption anyone would. They do their best to discredit you in court. My mother told me never to touch my face and since I was only going in for something so minor and he was so famous and I was just adding to the bridge where it sunk in, I didn't realize it was a set up. I'm so humiliated and embarrassed and my parents love me, I just couldn't tell them because it would break my heart to tell them that someone tried to hurt me and not only hurt me but stole all my dreams.

I cannot move my face to reflect to you what I am feeling. It just looks like a grimace. It hurts me.

The reflection of the self in the face is a human right. It has social impact to smile at others, to have a soft pretty expression. Mine is pulled and I can't relax my eyes now. It's so disturbing, I can't even have a thought and laugh about it, my expressions are not my own, they are the work of a madman.

If society says we don't matter, they are lying. We matter. We deserve happiness and we deserve to be productive members of society. We deserve the truth. We deserve public apology. We deserve our years back of human suffering. But, ask anyone who has ever been the victim of a wrong. Some things you have to give to yourself.

LISA DOUGLASS

When I think of America, I no longer think of justice, or freedom. I think of big business harvesting us, like

crops.

LISA DOUGLASS

They targeted us as if we were discards. Not worthy of a
life. But, I was a vital human being, even if I wasn't famous, I
was known in my own community for my irreverence and
style. And now, I know I was known for my beauty as well.

One of the many terrible parts of this has to do with their

gas-lighting and refusal to document each thing they did to us. We are prisoners of our faces until we unravel the mystery.

I was born beautiful. I was born safe. I was born for greatness. And so are you. I was born with an understanding of image. I visited Dr. Frankel three times to make sure he would be careful with my face. The lies he told me are easy to see in retrospect. That he was only adding a little to my bridge and if I didn't like it It was an easy fix. After he hurt me, he told me I could never be fixed.

My ex always tells me I have a flat bottom. But, it looks

extra flat here. Still, that's not the point. The point is I was so confident I never cared.

When I think of all the people I know whose lives have been hurt in the same way mine was, I see a great crime against humanity. Yes, we were stupid to get conned, but we didn't know they could pay to hide reviews. Predators prey on the goodness in people, not the corruption. The one thing I can see about each one of us, is our purity and goodness. We were innocent and kind. We were all very good people. Maybe our hearts were a little broken by the world. But, we were happy overall.

My friend made me this skateboard. I learned to ride it. I'm not very good, but it doesn't matter to me. The purpose wasn't in being good, it was in trying something new. For a hobby. For enjoyment.

The self that you don't understand is the one that can get you into the most trouble. I have always been surrounded by men. Women haven't always been kind to me, but they were around too. I always had an energy that drew attention when I walked through a room. When I was seventeen and just went to AA for the first time, I used to get stared at. I would hold my breath as I crossed the room. I never knew it was my beauty, because I was abused by my sister. She always told me how ugly I was. Men would have this insane reaction to me but I really didn't understand things like that. I thought they liked my fiery personality. But, it was more than that. Men like you because of your beauty.

This is Robert, the same boyfriend my friend Kelly had

before she knew me. I would have married Robert. We planned to get married but he couldn't stay sober and went in and out of rehabs while I was in graduate school teaching the New Jim Crow and fiction. I have never been so in love with anyone, but like a burning planet plummeting to earth, Robert is digging up gold in the mountains, in between

getting high.

WHEN YOU ARE IN A LAWSUIT, THEY
COMB YOUR SOCIAL MEDIA. THEY WILL
SHOW THE JURY THAT I PUT UP PHOTOS

OVER THE THREE YEARS I HAD BEEN
BOTCHED. I MADE A MOVIE TO
PROTECT OTHERS, I TRIED TO KEEP MY
SPIRIT ALIVE AND I HID IN FILM
SCHOOL AND LEARNED TO USE A
CAMERA, BECAUSE I COULD NO
LONGER BE ME IN MY LIFE AS THE
PERSON I HAD BEEN.

AND MARIA HOVSEPIAN AND ADAM
ROBINSON WOULD USE THAT AGAINST
ME IN COURT. THE DISFIGURATION OF
A SPIRIT, THE RUINING OF A LIFE, WAS
GOING TO BE DISCREDITED BY TWO
ATTORNEYS THAT HATED ME. AND I
HAD TO BE STRONGER THAN THEY
WERE TO GET IT TO A JURY TO PROVE
MY CASE, WITHOUT MONEY, WITHOUT
A LEGAL TEAM AND WITHOUT MY
PRETTY FACE.

This is my friend Suzanne. One of the best girlfriends I've
ever had. We went to class together at UCLA when I
decided to go back and get my degree. I think she is a
lawyer now. She always told me I would be okay. She was a
very good friend and understood my personal demons came
from childhood things. A sister's meanness made me strong

in the world, but frightened of relationships. And it made
me not know my own power. I had finally known myself and
fully accepted my uniqueness and was filled with hope
when Dr. Frankel destroyed me.

Be careful of the predators, they will try to kill you and
you'll be saying are you safe? and They will do it anyway,
Just to prove they can.

This is my friend Justin. He moved to Germany recently. I almost moved him in here at one point. We were very close friend before this happened to me.

Never take your beauty for granted.

This is my friend Sonja Kinski. She told me to be careful about surgery and after I got it done and it was a disaster, she never spoke to me again. I just didn't know how to talk about it and she used to get really upset with me for all kinds of reasons. Including I reminded her of her mother. We had a complex friendship. She used to tell me she thought I was probably good in bed. I asked how she knew and she said she could just tell. She told me once she had a long Caligula. I told her Caligula was a Porno from the 1970s. It was called the columella. In my deposition they insinuate I didn't know the meaning of a columella. But, Andrew Frankel's photos had them and it was a feature of my face I loved. No one has ever made me laugh as hard as Sonja.

I can't make these expressions with my eyes anymore
because Dr. Frankel disabled my levator superioris aleque nasi
muscle---this is the main muscle of human expression and it
lifts the lip and runs from the eyes to the mouth. My face is

never relaxed because it feels paralyzed. I can move my cheeks only with great effort. I never knew how easy I had it or how someone would try to harm you. We have a letter from a girl who worked for Andrew Frankel and she told us that sometimes it seemed he hurt people on purpose. That is my contention too. He stole our smiles. Our ability to be in the world in front of the camera. He stole that piece of us that never knew violence can come at any time. In many forms.

This is my dear sweet dad. He is the smartest, kindest
man I have ever known. He studied at USC's Medical School
and got a full ride because his organic chemistry scores were
off the chart. He tells the funniest stories. Like the time he
needed a lemonade when he was out selling bibles. He is pure

and charming and I've never met anyone like him. When I was little he told me not to take advantage of men and I never did. But both my parents always thought I was beautiful.

This is my beautiful Mother. I should find her modeling photos so you understand her beauty is both elegant and timeless. I'm sad our faces don't look like one another's anymore.

I just didn't know how to tell her someone ruined what she and my dad and god gave me, by trusting someone untrustworthy. I could be dead I guess, but I know she loves me anyway, even if I'm not pretty anymore and the camera no longer loves me.

This is my long ago writing partner, Nicole Kelly. She is a miracle of a person. She felt the same way about grad school as

I did. That no one got us. We wrote a short script about my life in LA doing weird jobs and it landed as a Quarter-Finalist in the first contest we entered.

This is the other Christian. He was my writing partner and my boyfriend or I dated him or whatever complexity that was. This is the only photograph in the book of after my botched surgery and two reconstructions. If I didn't include Christian it wouldn't make sense. He saw me when I was badly botched and still liked me even though I was very disfigured. He is one of the only people I can be around for days and days and never get sick of him. We are not dating anymore due to the complexities of my lawsuit and my lack of time but I do love him very much and hope he writes the next great American Novel, right after I do. Because he is a brilliant genius.

LISA DOUGLASS

LISA DOUGLASS

This is my friend CC Wright, he has been a really good friend to me under the craziest circumstances. He is one of my favorite people. He moved away and I never see him, but he remains in my heart for always. We had this fight once when we were shopping for furniture. I can't even remember what it was about, but he stormed out and I stood there not even knowing what happened. We didn't speak for months, and then we made up like it never happened. CC took me to see Depeche Mode at the Staples Center. We had box seats and sang and danced to every song.

LISA DOUGLASS

LISA DOUGLASS

Here's a letter I wrote to Michael Quick of USC Keck.

Mr. Quick —

Your statements that you defend your
administrators and that safety and well-being is

143

your number one goal in the recent lawsuits of USC students being violated by your own Gynecologist, has me curious about the use of student residents and fellows in unaccredited facilities scattered across Beverly Hills that use deception to allow operations and disfigurement for "mandated research" and "licensure" by USC students, Clerks, Interns.

I am copying all of the botched victims of Dr. Andrew Frankel, MD and Jay Calvert, MD wherein you knowingly use outside ambulatory care centers for certain "tests" and "research" without patient consent, knowing Calvert has been arrested for a felony and has a long history of damaging patients by conducting un-consented to research upon their faces—including tissue scaffolding and implantation of fibrin sealant. And Dr. Andrew Frankel, MD wherein a statewide and USC wide coverup of his actions to let USC students conduct dangerous and facial altering, destructive, non therapeutic research damaging organs and body parts without regard for patient well being has been underway for decades. Hush agreements issued by these two doctors, aside, letting students conduct Vaginal Wet Mounts and inexplicably catheterization of the patients in two outside facilities that USC knowingly uses for "certain accreditation purposes" is a flagrant and disturbing violation of Human Experimentation laws and regulations.

Targeting rhinoplasty patients because the

ACGME now requires 6 rhinoplasties before being accredited, so once you lure one person, you "make the most" of the case.

Your apology should go to the BCC's on this list as well as you have destroyed lives with this undertaking and I'm thinking you personally should be named in our lawsuit for ignoring all of my letters even after I informed you of Dan Shapiro's heartless statements that USC students can conduct research on anyone they want to without consent.

I have copied Kimberly Kirchmeyer of the Board of Medicine who thankfully re-reported Dr. Andrew Frankel's previous malpractice which the Medical Board had been hiding from the public to allow your covert operations.

I will now publish each and every letter you ignored for the public to see that not only don't you care, but your recent admissions publically are a total fraud. You do not care about human suffering of victims. In fact, claiming you do in the press is an outrage to the numerous victims I am copying on this letter.

Lisa Douglass

The American Academy of Facial Plastic and Reconstructive Surgeons are also responsible. They allow mandated human research that is non-therapeutic to the patient. When I called Fatima Porter-El—she looked me up in a Fellow Database and told me that Andrew Frankel did not conduct my surgery. Sim Choroomi did. I thanked her because I had suffered for over two years with no idea that a student did my surgery.

Others have called her and she has lied about the existence of a fellow database. I am attaching the evidence at the end of this book and her letter to me and my letter back to her after I found out.

Max Subin of the Beverly Hills Police Department said it is not in his jurisdiction to investigate and he took Detective Berger

146

off the case and told him to close the investigation without ever going to Lasky Clinic. Max Subin single-handedly told me I walked in on my own volition and he would not investigate that the Lasky Clinic was not accredited to have fellowships or fellows conducting surgery on the property. I have an audio of his statements, which include Kimberly Kirchmeyer's misrepresentation to him that I had requested investigation for duty of care, when I did not. I asked for investigation of falsification of records and aiding and abetting unlicensed students.

Sim Choroomi, who did the procedure along with other
residents was not licensed to perform any surgery in the states.

USC has since removed their Surgical Skills Clerkship Manual,
but I had it printed so I took a few screenshots and entered
them into this manual at the end. The main thing to remember

is it says the students take a test at a HIGH-
STAKES OFFSITE
FACILITY.

Additionally, after I sued and got a local television
reporter involved, the producer started hunting around.
We both watched as USC hid all associations with
Andrew Frankel from the internet. Now they are hiding
their own surgical manual and removed it from the
Internet too.

In case you are a victim. Bad people happen. But you
have to know, you are not alone. It's a lot of us. Smart,
vital, beautiful people who were harmed and had thought
we were careful.

LISA DOUGLASS

ABOUT THE AUTHOR

Lisa Douglass is a writer and an actor who lives in Los
Angeles. She likes taking photos and loves puppies and her
parents. She became a political activist after USC students
illegally operated on her face in a clinic not accredited as a
training facility. The predator doctor that hurt her and many
others is still practicing on faces at Lasky Clinic, using USC
students, residents and fellows rather than doing the
procedures himself.

Following is some of my attempts to get justice and my own records. I cut and pasted them in the first version of the book but no one could read it, so here they are and I have removed the tiny photos of the letters as I am not allowed to publish things the public cannot read.

Ms. Douglass, (November 22, 2017)

Thank you for your email and for contacting the Medical Board of California (Board) regarding the complaints you filed against Dr. Frankel. Based upon the information you have provided, I will have staff review your complaint file to determine if the information you have provided is new information, specifically regarding the unlicensed individuals performing surgeries. Our records indicate that you filed a complaint regarding the care you received and that the information and medical records were reviewed by a medical consultant. After review, the Board determined it did not have evidence to pursue disciplinary action against Dr. Frankel. However, I will have staff review the information you have provided below and determine if this additional information is new information regarding your complaint.

Thank you for bringing to my attention the problems you have encountered when contacting the Board. I am sorry that you felt that a member of our staff was rude to you and that you did not receive return calls. Please be aware I will look into these issues as well.

A member or our Enforcement Management team will reply to you regarding the information you have provided. Again, thank you for contacting the Board and bringing this matter to my attention.

Sincerely,

Kimberly Kirchmeyer
Executive Director
Medical Board of California
2005 Evergreen Street, Suite 1200
Sacramento, CA 95815

Dear Ms. Douglass, (

Thank you for your email and inquiry to the Medical Board of California (Board). In response to your question regarding the reason for the closure of your case against Dr. Frankel, please see the attached letters sent to you on August 2, 2017 and January 26, 2018, explaining why your case was closed. Both letters explain that the Board was unable to prove that there was a departure from the standard of care and therefore the Board could not take action against Dr. Frankel.

Your email below also asks why information was removed from Dr. Frankel's record regarding a malpractice judgment. Please be aware that pursuant to Business and Professions Code section 2027 as of January 1, 2013, certain information over ten years old had to be removed from a physician's website profile. Legislation was subsequently changed that removed this restriction from the Board's posting requirements. Therefore, the Board was able to again add Dr. Frankel's malpractice judgment to his website profile.

The Board understands you are dissatisfied with the outcome of your complaint against Dr. Frankel. However, the Board must be able to prove by clear and convincing evidence that a violation of the Medical Practice Act occurred in order to take disciplinary action against any licensee.

Again, thank you for contacting the Board.

Sincerely,

Kimberly Kirchmeyer
Executive Director
Medical Board of California
2005 Evergreen Street, Suite 1200
Sacramento, CA 95815
(916) 263-2389 (May 5, 2018)

Dear Ms. Kirchmeyer, (Medical Board)

I am copying all of the people harmed by this doctor. We still are asking why you closed the

USC, AAFPRS and Lasky complaints without investigation—as in I have no paper record of your investigation findings or of closing them . We were innocent victims and we'd like to know why.

They individually are very happy you have put back this person's malpractice judgement on your site to protect the public.

The necrosis case, which you closed without investigation.
The pneumothorax case which you closed without investigation.
The man who doctor Frankel filed a Restraining order after mutilating his mouth instead of fixing the nose.
The man who ended up in a mental institution so he did not kill himself are all on this list.

I have carefully reviewed the Medical Practice Act. None of us have comprehensive records, none of the records are accurate—we have had to gather one another's records and try to find out which of the procedures were left off, conducted on others and are under enormous pressure to find out what was done to disfigure and disable our mouths and noses. There was no justification for 26 additional procedures and working on the mouth and cheek in the course of an augmentation of the bridge or the removal of 90 percent of my nose during augmentation procedure for the bridge of my nose (adding procedure). I have records from each new doctor who had to try to rebuild my nose verifying

155

that the mouth muscles were cut, the septum shortened the nostrils cut off and moved inward and downward among many other procedures conducted without justification as I was going for a larger nose and each procedure conducted was to shorten and make smaller and I was an actress and he wrote down his intent to deviate from the plan.
The plan is to give her a septocolumellar suture so I don't have to augment her bridge. Showing knowledge of what i want and intent to do the opposite, which is a violent departure from the covenant of patient-physician communication, agreement and trust. And shows intent to kill my life, livelihood and personal goals. I met with three other doctors before my procedure to substantiate my claims, even one at **Lasky Cllinic, Behrooz Torkian who states what i wanted: a larger bridge and a wider tip.**

Each new surgeon's records show that my own records are falsified and not comprehensive. So the burden is on the patient and these are all violations of the Medical Practice Act you insinuate had no deviations.

Each additional procedure was left off my operating report. No emergencies took place. Dr. Frankel's defense counsel admitted he didn't do the surgery, but told each of us, he would perform the surgery completely and fully as my record will reveal.

All my tissue was removed and then billed Medicare for which is a breach of fiduciary duty because the doctor gets paid the more procedures he allows the students to do to the rhinoplasty patient. These practices are horrific abuse of a human life. Dr. Frankel admits moving the nostrils does not look good, so why is he letting students perform it routinely on actresses and others to disable their mouths?

My new doctors all stated my nostrils were cut from my muscles and moved and sewn to a lower location —all missing from my operative report.

Informed consent doctrine under Cobbs also now includes Perry v. Shaw, which is when one substantially deviates from the plan and does what was specifically asked not to be done to harm the patient.

We had no informed consent with regards to the students operating or fellows or residents who took a test on our faces for USC or had rights to touch our vagina's or catheterize us from the USC's **Skills and Thrills Manual** where students take a test on a patient in a high-stakes off site secret location.

There is no therapeutic privilege when someone is an actress and asks that no other changes be made to the nose or face, but then that greed forces them to mutilate the face. That is performance of non-therapeutic research that does not benefit the victim. Closing USC Keck, AAFPRS, and Lasky Clinic's who runs an illegal fellowship, not accredited by the ACGME shows state interest in collusion to deceive the public.

I'd like the record of the final investigation in these cases too.

Thank you for your attention.
Lisa Douglass (May 6th, 2017)

Bullshit letter from the Board who allows students to try out cleft lip repairs on healthy people without ever investigating.

Dear Ms. Douglass, (May 5, 2018)

Thank you for your email and inquiry to the Medical Board of California (Board). In response to your question regarding the reason for the closure of your case against Dr. Frankel, please see the attached letters sent to you on August 2, 2017 and January 26, 2018, explaining why your case was closed. Both letters explain that the Board was unable to prove that there was a departure from the standard of care and therefore the Board could not take action against Dr. Frankel.

Your email below also asks why information was removed from Dr. Frankel's record regarding a malpractice judgment. Please be aware that pursuant to Business and Professions Code section 2027 as of January 1, 2013, certain information over ten years old had to be removed from a physician's website profile. Legislation was subsequently changed that removed this restriction from the Board's posting requirements. Therefore, the Board was able to again add Dr. Frankel's malpractice judgment to his website profile.

The Board understands you are dissatisfied with the outcome of your complaint against Dr. Frankel. However, the Board must be able to prove by clear and convincing evidence that a violation of the Medical Practice Act occurred in order to take disciplinary action against any licensee.

Again, thank you for contacting the Board.

Sincerely,

Kimberly Kirchmeyer
Executive Director
Medical Board of California
2005 Evergreen Street, Suite 1200
Sacramento, CA 95815
          (916) 263-2389

Dear Sirs, (HHS Letter Federal Government)

It has come to the attention that the following agencies are misusing Human Subjects by implanting Medical Devices for Research without an IRB oversight board and our medical Board Refuses to Investigate. The president of the Board says students are licensed without consideration that we were lied to and misled about them actually conducting surgeries upon our persons. I am disabled from many students cutting off my mouth muscles in the course of a cosmetic nose surgery to add to the top of my nose. I was an actress. I have been disfigured and paid out of pocket over $100,000 for reconstructive surgeries.

The doctor has refused to tell any of us what was done to us and we have begged and one man ended up in a mental hospital.
We all went to an outside clinic, Lasky Clinic and though they are not accredited to conduct fellowships, they duped us and used students, who disfigured us by implantation of medical devices made by Ethicon, Endo Surgery through the sponsoring institution USC Keck and Keck Institute of Applied Science.

We have evidence that USC is using outside facilities to get their students accredited and target rhinoplasty patients as the ACGME now requires 6 rhinoplasties to be performed before getting licensed. We are in court and the Medical Board has just re-reported Dr. Andrew Frankel for Malpractice who was the doctor who lured us to ensure public disclosure and hopefully to help others from being permanently maimed.

Lasky Clinic is an ambulatory care center that USC uses without regulatory IRB oversight.

They are implanting investigational devices without human consent and without an experimental bill of rights or proper consent as these devices permanently destroy human structure of the mouth and nose. We are numerous and found that you do investigations in these matters. Can you please investigate that Dan Shapiro of Keck's Clinical Compliance and Human Researh Board claims to be "allowed" to have students conduct research in outside clinics without a patient consent or bill of rights or an Investigational Plan or Human oversight board? This is abuse of Human Subjects in Research and we would appreciate you investigate Lasky Clinic and USC for their mandated research policies with no oversight board or Approved Investigational Plans.

Thank you very much. There are 11 of us, if you would like me to provide the disfigurement and proof none of us signed an experimental bill of rights or were provided with one, though we found USC Keck to have conducted research in a publication bragging about the lack of a Human Reseach IRB oversight board and has admitted the surgeries were non-therapeutic and "look bad".

I have attached the documents of interest. USC admitting to using the outside facility even though it is unlawful for fellowships and the JAMA publication to lower our nostrils and destroy facial mobility without proper consent.

We have involved the press as this is the illegal use of Human Research Subjects akin to Nazi Germany's human experimentation policies.

Thank you for your consideration, this is an abuse of funds, as they get Medicare money to do this to unsuspecting innocent parties.

I have reported them repeatedly to the board, who routinely closes our complaints without review.

Thank you for your time.

Lisa Douglass
323-346-5175 (May 6th)

Ms Kirchmeyer, (May 17th)

You are splitting hairs and claiming any of my claims had to do with quality of care to protect a violent and dangerous doctor.

You are a known corrupt agency who does this but there are so many of us disfigured and I never once claimed quality of care. I claimed deliberate battery, falsification of records and the like.
I'm assuming we will have to sue you for your absolute greed and refusal to protect the public. I have done everything in my power to inform the press, to document your complete bastardization

of the laws that are in force to protect the citizens, and you close the complaint and will absolutely have to be confronted publically about this—you hid his malpractice and gave no real reason except some law that wasn't even cited, showing a statewide coverup with intent to harm citizens. Because each day you do nothing, women and children and men are being experimented on as if this is Nazi Germany and your lack of doing anything, will leave blood on your own hands when someone dies and when the press comes calling, you will not be able to say you didn't know. I have all the records. I don't appreciate you closing any complaint regarding quality of care as I know I never checked that box, in fact I am looking at the boxes I checked and have many falsified records and much evidence that you are not investigating? Why? You leave men and women almost dead and XXXX went to a mental institution and you refuse to investigate? That you stand without a conscience in the face of a monster and side with him shows you to be an agent of the state looking to harm its citizens. That is state action. I have a public recording of exactly what you told Max Subin of the Beverly Hills Department and you are absolutely going to be documented all over the internet for your failure to act. And when the judge sees you in court he will ask what box I was supposed to check—because to lie to a public official about what I asked you to investigate is going to come haunt you because now I have documentation that you lied to the police.

As totally cutting off all facial muscles in the course of a surgery, is outside the standard of care and had this been your mother or daughter, you would be aghast. But, I guess since it wasn't you, I can only count on the courts to enforce your total refusal to help the public who has been targeted and mutilated as you stood by and did nothing. I hope to see you in the history books, like those that allowed Joseph Mengele to act out experimentations on human subjects to destroy their psyches and their lives. It will be you, a woman, who enforced the ruthless mutilation.

You are not human.

Lisa Douglass

Hello Lisa: (November 15th letter from the AAFPRS)

Thank you for sending the information. As I indicated in our phone conversation yesterday fellows are allowed to perform surgery as our fellowships are not observership fellowships.

I will send your information on for review. If you need to be contacted your phone number and email address may be used for that purpose.

My sincerest heartfelt empathy is with you.

"Tap into the unlimited mind of creation and draw from it the right thoughts, plans and actions that will lead you to your ultimate success."

Fatima Porter EL Mitchell
Fellowship Program Manager
(703) 299-9291 ext. 228
(703) 299-8898 (FAX)

Dear Ms. Douglass,

Please see the attached letter regarding your request for your medical file.

Sincerely,

Steve Jurich (November 30, 2017)
AAFPRS

EDUCATIONAL AND RESEARCH FOUNDATION FOR THE AMERICAN ACADEMY OF FACIAL PLASTIC AND RECONSTRUCTIVE SURGERY
310 S. Henry Street, Alexandria, VA 22314   Phone (703) 299-9291   Fax (703) 299-8898   www.aafprs.org

November 29, 2017

Ms. Lisa Douglass
101 South Sycamore Avenue, #5
Los Angeles, CA 90036

Dear Ms. Douglass:

Thank you for your letter of November 21, 2017 (emailed on November 22, 2017).

You request your medical file. Neither our Academy, nor its Educational and Research Foundation, have any medical records concerning your care. Therefore, we are unable to provide the information you request.

We note that your letter addresses a number of other patients, research, and other issues. We do not believe it would advance any dialogue to attempt a line by line rebuttal. Suffice it to say respectfully that, to the extent we have any access to information about those subjects, our view of the facts is different from yours.

We are mindful of your authorization that we might contact Dr. Frankel. Accordingly, we are sharing with him our exchange of emails and correspondence.

Sincerely,

Steven Jurish
Executive Vice President & CEO
AAFPRS and AAFPRS Foundation

Dear Fatima, (November 15, 2017)

Thank you for your help today and for your honesty in telling me that the fellows are supposed to perform the surgery. This has been a two year process of being lied to and searching and searching. I did not know that the fellow performed or would perform my surgery. I carefully vetted my surgeon and he told us the second form referred to anesthesiolgists and nurses—not the fellow.

They used deceit to gain my consent. The fellow that operated removed all my mouth muscles and they lied to me about it for two years saying I was old. I've been devastated professionally, financially and psychologically by this deceit.

I went to have my bridge filled in only. Dr. Frankel wrote the intent to do the opposite and then let his fellow destroy my face. The fact that I was misled and used to train a fellow is against my rights as a human being. This deceit was long standing. I went to meet with Frankel three times to remove the filler in my nose in order to place it back in my nose. I am attaching the operative report and the letter from Sim Choroomi lying to me telling me they made my nose substantially larger. I lost my career, my standing in my community and am friends with a member of the city council who said this ghost surgery practice occurs all the time. Please know, My life was ruined in order for one person to "learn" without my consent or knowledge. Lasky Clinic and Dr. Frankel told me the assistants were anesthesiologists on the second form. This dangerous doctor deliberately allows fellows to perform without our consent. He and the fellows training on our faces are ruining our lives.

I was an actress and had just been on TV and Alfre Woodard told me how pretty I was. Then they disfigured me. You knew of this practice as a fellowship participant, but I did not.I carefully vetted my surgeon. They disabled my mouth and I can barely brush my teeth or speak and they lied about it for two full years.

Please see these forms and please understand I have been contacted by humans ruined by this Clinic and this doctor by people all over the world. We are deeply disturbed that this practice is done without our consent.
I am attaching my xrays of my mouth muscles severed permanently by this student fellow. My life was ruined.

I kept asking Dr. Frankel what happened to me and he told me I was old. This is the most terrible thing that can ever happen to a person and no one would tell me what happened to me. But they knew. Please note in the medical records the use of 'we'. should not be a shock since you said they are supposed to perform this procedure. But, additionally they shortened and cut off all my muscles, instead of buildiing my nose, for training. I lost my career. Please look me up, I have a huge following. My name online is Girltown.

When I asked why my mouth had become long, a second fellow Christian Paquet filmed Dr. Frankel chopping off the footplates of another patient to show me it is tissue I don't really need. The footplates are attached to the mouth muscles.

Dr. Frankel filed a restraining order against a patient for complaining. He is highly unethical and this practice without consent, when we chose the best doctor we could afford because our professions counted on it, is extremely disturbing.

We were additionally placed in a study spearheaded by Sim Choroomi and this was performed on me as an experiment without my consent.
Thank you for your time,
Lisa Douglass

Dear Mr. Quick, (USC KECK DEAN) December 13, 2017 (Laura Courte and Dan Shapiro were copied)

Early last month I was in contact with the LA Times due to being disfigured, used in research by one of your students without my consent and not at a training hospital but an outside faciliity called Lasky Clinic..

Not only did I find the JAMA article that was published after all of my mouth muscles were cut off, but when I contacted Dan Shapiro, he got highly upset, claimed to not know the doctor in question, claimed he would research what my claim was to find out if any patient protocol was in place for protecting students and never got back to me. The students bragging about this research claiming no conflicts of interest, were Christian Paquet and Sim Choroomi. The doctor was and is Dr. Andrew Frankel.

My father graduated from USC and I was disfigured by a student, at the very least instead of having a private investigator call me, taking this seriously or being at the very least apologetic would have been the appropriate protocol, but hiding in the bush is not.

USC was named on the consent forms and this was a curriculum for your students, but we were all misled that the doctor that we carefully vetted was going to be performing the surgery. There are a lot of patients and the doctor who did this to us, was in an outside clinic acting under your auspices without being regulated or without being a training facility.

When I call your office, your secretary threatened me, which I don't feel is appropriate.

Dan Shapiro said the students were allowed to conduct research upon us without our consent, but that is against federal law.

I'd like you to know, I gave you as USC the benefit of the doubt, but Laura LaCorte and Dan Shapiro have treated me with complete disregard.

Thanks for listening,

Lisa Douglass

February 13, 2018 letter to Dan Shapiro of USC's Clinical Compliance (Michael Quick and Laura Lacorte were copied)

So, it is now February, you have pretended to know nothing. But, now the defense attorneys have claimed Dr. Frankel is a paid proctor for USC. Therefore all of the botched victims and their families see you as responsible. You knew as much as the people who supported Harvey Weinstein knew. You allowed us to be stolen from, disfigured and our lives destroyed.
Legally, Proctors cannot know the patients and cannot deceive them or meet with them or touch them, yet Frankel charged for repeated procedures and then used students again while you knew. HE met with us and deceived us and as a member of the public, I asked for your acknowledgement and you treated me like i was inhuman, after I have already been used in a research paper. I asked about the safety protocol and was told you don't know Dr. Frankel.

Dan Shapiro's lied to me and got angry when his mouth muscles were not cut off and his face destroyed by a student who could not pass his exams. USC's historical tactics to hurt the public is going down in history and now legally. I am an activist and a huge number of disfigured patients your students botched without our consent or knowledge and they sent me their operative reports and we are upset that you did nothing. I tell you, you will speak to a Judge, you will explain how you knew and let us be destroyed. Like in Larry Nassar's case, you took government funds to destroy lives.

USC should remember, more people have influence through writing, through video footage and through testimony from the children of men and women you have destroyed.
You are not providing a function to the state to disfigure people by allowing them to be botched by students for a curriculum. You destroyed our lives financially and legitimately and Dan Shapiro and Mr. Quick knew—they have known the entire time.
.
USC has a problem on its hands.

May 5th, 2017
Dear Ms. Kirchmeyer,

Thank you for your response and for re-reporting the malpractice that Dr. Frankel was found guilty of in a court of law. As I have stated numerous times, my case is one of many whereas Dr. Frankel conducted research without consent and without an IRB oversight board.

As for finding no evidence of wrong doing, let me remind you that 26 un-consented, un-neccessary

and disabling procedures were performed by USC
students "taking a test" at Lasky Clinic under the
purview of Dr. Frankel's role as a proctor without
my consent and these procedures were
deliberately enacted to disable my mouth;
Including but not limited to Cleft Lip repair
procedures, maxillary jaw procedures and my
cheek being inexplicably sutured to my nostrils—
during the course of a cosmetic rhinoplasty
augmentation of the bridge of my nose. And as an
actress how this would affect my psyche and well-
being and that you close complaints of people who
had Pneumothorax and Necrosis stating no
departure from standard of care exists, when you
and USC knowingly target rhinoplasty patients in
private outside clinics is baffling to me.

That you find falsified records of a criminal with
fraudulent reviews reported by the public and
reported on television on ReviewFraud.org—that
anything this Doctor states, or that you would take
anything this doctor states to be true and take
them as truth and refuse to take any other
evidence, including my new doctors proving Dr.
Frankel removed most of my nose (lied about it)
and cut off my mouth muscles and left both items
and many other items off the report, I have to say
as a member of the public, whereas Dr. Frankel is
cutting off mouth muscles routinely, then filing
restraining orders against patients. And the
powerful situation whereas no disfigured patient
can find the emotional strength or financial
strength with which to sue and that your own

president admitted on record that "the students are licensed," the state is responsible for this by turning a blind eye to the deliberate actions Dr. Frankel takes to lure and harm his patients without intent of conducting the procedures at all.

Additionally, we have evidence that the fellows can conduct procedures and so can residents, both illegally and fraudulently being kept from the public and that they are mandated to conduct research upon our persons while Frankel brags about how he is not watched by an oversight board and the procedures he conducts "does not look good" therefore un-therapeutic research. To find no wrong doings shows your complicit actions to allow the targeting, disfiguring and knowingly denigrating inaction of a statewide issue that is damaging the public and against all constitutional rights of the patient. That your president shamelessly stated on the record that it doesn't matter that we didn't consent, shows a statewide coverup, whereas you sit docile at the helm.

I do not accept your dismissiveness about our human rights whereas we were disfigured purposefully or that we were never told a team of untrained, unlicensed students would be operating, without ever having performed procedures to get their ACGME accreditation. I find you and Dr. Dev to be criminally responsible for Crimes against Humanity a la Nazi Germany where you are targeting good American people to "conduct experiments on" and you allow it, encourage it and then close complaints without investigation just because "you can".

I do not accept your lack of empathy as anything less than state sponsored butchery of human beings with rights and feelings and am disgusted by the board's inaction.

My friend XXXX XXXXXXXXX heard back from you and he ended up in a mental institution and I hear from victims daily and you are responsible. I hold you accountable and will never rest until you actually investigate this dangerous criminal who disfigures then laughs at his patients after destroying their mouths, cheeks and noses for no other reason than he can charge for repeat procedures to Medicare who pays for the fellows.

You are responsible and i will never rest until you stand before a jury and tell them why you refused to investigate after people BEGGED you to do so for the sake of all future human beings and citizens who come to California for rhinoplasties, to have a better life, not to be permanently maimed by students without credentials or rights to touch the body.

That the ACGME claims that no rhinoplasty patient goes to a training facility and that you are secretly aidiing and abetting the covert actions of USC to use private paying patients as human guinea pigs, knowing the entire legal system is against them and that the ACGME now requires these students conduct 6 procedures before being licensed and that I had 26 un-consented to procedures, shows the state supported human experimentation by this doctor is very unsafe and people are risking their lives due to pure American Greed and covert fraudulent deception.

Your inaction shows collusion to destroy lives and your lack of care for human safety astounds the conscience. I for one paid over $100,000 to try to get fixed and still am paralyzed in my face as it was sutured to a lower position without this fact being anywhere on any operative report. These students did this without regard for my well-being and Frankel lied repeatedly to me and many others that "he honored the wishes of his patients and conducts the procedure fully and completely." Then in Bold type **Dr. Frankel does the surgery**. That you don't see this consumer fraud as worthy of investigation or wrong doing shows your support of the criminal and not the victim.

I find you to be a state agency that laughs at those who are harmed and that your time will come, just as Harvey Weinstein's did and Bill Cosby's did. Because this is human trafficking, killing souls and destruction of lives.

I am astonished at your indecency, the Indecency of Frankel and of the Indecency of USC's Dan Shapiro who claims these students can conduct research upon our persons without consent any time they want to.

The last lawyer I spoke to said not only is this national news but this is criminal coverup.

Lisa Douglass

February 27, 2018 (Letter from the AAFPRS Lawyer)

On behalf of the American Academy of Facial Plastic and Reconstructive Surgery, I respectfully reply to your recent email to the Academy's Mr. Jurich. I must share with you that the California subpoena to which you refer is unavailing in Virginia where it was served. I'll also share that the Academy does not have the documents you seek.

Sent from my BlackBerry - the most secure mobile device

Thomas W. Rhodes | Attorney at Law

404-815-3551 *phone*
404-685-6851 *fax*
www.sgrlaw.comTRHODES@sgrlaw.com

Promenade, Suite 3100
1230 Peachtree Street, N.E.
Atlanta, Georgia 30309-3592

Dear Attorney Rhodes, (March 8th, 2018)

Spoilation of evidence is a federal crime. I will
inform the judge on the 13th that you will not
comply with my requests for my own medical file.
Additionally, Fatima Porter-El looked up my
records in the Fellow Database and informed me
that Sim Choroomi was my surgeon.
I want my own Medical Files and will ask the court
to hold you in contempt for your refusal to oblige.

Lisa Douglass

Keck Medical Center of USC

OFFICE OF INTEGRATED RISK MANAGEMENT
Keck Hospital of USC/USC Norris Cancer Hospital
USC Care Medical Group
USC Verdugo Hills Hospital

Dear Lisa Douglass,

We want to assure you that Keck Medicine of USC strives to provide excellent care and service for our patients and the community. We appreciate you sharing your concerns about the care you received at the Lasky Clinic in December 2015 and we have investigated this to the best of our ability in order to understand the circumstances surrounding the event. According to your letter to the university, you have been "seeking a solution for the two years since (your) surgery" and believe that your DNA and tissue was stolen for research purposes.

We certainly can appreciate the frustration you feel when the quality or level of care you expect is not met. However, there appears to be some confusion with regards to the relationship that USC has with Dr. Andrew Frankel and the Lasky Clinic and we would like to take this opportunity to address that.

Lasky Clinic
The only relationship that the USC Tina and Rick Caruso Department of Otolaryngology-Head and Neck Surgery has with the Lasky Clinic is as an academic affiliate. This affiliation is narrowly limited to certain accreditation functions and does not include a resident rotation or any broader agreement with the Lasky Clinic. As a result, we do not have access to the medical records, policies, or any information regarding the services that were provided.

Andrew Frankel, MD
Dr. Andrew Frankel is a private practice facial plastics surgeon whose relationship to the Keck School of Medicine was limited to a voluntary faculty position. As a voluntary faculty, Dr. Frankel had no employment relationship with Keck Medicine of USC, which includes our University medical group and hospitals. Dr. Frankel was provided this limited, voluntary position in order for the Lasky Clinic to have a facial plastic and reconstructive surgery fellowship, however, Dr. Frankel did not and does not have an official role teaching our residents.

Fellows
Christian Paquet, MD. Dr. Christian Paquet is a former USC resident who became a Fellow at the Lasky Clinic, however, he did not provide services at the Lasky Clinic through any kind of official rotation that was sponsored through the University.

Sim Choroomi, MD. Dr. Choroomi was a Lasky Fellow from Australia but we have no information on this individual as he was not part of any program sponsored by USC.

University of Southern California
1800 San Pablo Street, Los Angeles, California 90033 • Tel: 323 442 5968 • Fax 323 442 9988

Keck Medical
Center of USC

Summary

We're hopeful that this clarifies our relationship and the fact that Keck Medicine of USC had no direct clinical oversight of this program or of the practices at the Lasky Clinic.

We appreciate you giving us the opportunity to address your concerns and encourage you to contact us at (323) 442-5968 if you have any additional questions.

Thank you,

Josh Hyatt, D.H.Sc., MHL., CPHRM, FASHRM
Executive Director
Office of Integrated Risk Management
Keck Medicine of USC

LISA DOUGLASS

RESEARCH/SCHOLARLY PAPER

All fellows must submit a research paper as part of the fellowship experience. Clinical, basic science, meta-analysis and systematic review papers are acceptable. Prior to submitting the paper through the Fellowship Database fellows should have received feedback from the Fellowship Research Review Subcommittee (FRRS) on submitting an acceptable paper. Fellows should not proceed too far with their research without submitting an abstract in the event the title or research is not acceptable. Papers must be reviewed and approved for submission by the Fellowship Director, through the Fellowship Database. Guidelines for writing research/scholarly papers and *Information for Authors* from the *JAMA Facial Plastic Surgery* can be obtained from the AAFPRS Foundation fellowship office.

Papers should be submitted through the Fellowship Database June 1st of the fellowship year **or the year immediately following training completion to qualify for the Roe or Gillies Awards**. Any fellow not uploading a paper by the end of their fellowship year must submit a progress report through the Fellowship Database. The progress report is not in lieu of a paper submission but in addition to. Any fellow not submitting a research paper or progress report form by June 30th **will not** be eligible to receive a fellowship certificate.

AWARDS DESCRIPTIONS

- The John Orlando Roe Award is named after the surgeon who accomplished the first rhinoplasty in 1887. This honor includes a certificate and a monetary award of $1,000 and is presented each year to the fellow in the fellowship program who submits the best clinical research paper written during his/her fellowship.

- The Sir Harold Delf Gillies award is named for Sir Harold Delf Gillies who was a British Otolaryngologist who in September 1917 described the tubed pedicle flap. Dr. Gillies frequently visited the U.S. and lectured widely to surgeons of various specialties and was given the title "Father of Plastic Surgery." A certificate and a monetary award of $1,000 is presented each year to the fellow in the fellowship program who submits the best basic science research paper written during his/her fellowship.

All papers are evaluated anonymously by the FRRS and must receive subcommittee approval in order to satisfy this requirement. The FRRS may include comments or suggestions for improvement, which will be noted on the letter of

9

Andrew S. Frankel, MD, FACS
201 South Lasky Drive
Beverly Hills, CA 90212-3647
(310) 552-2173
(310) 552-0418 (FAX)

UNIVERSITY AFFILIATION:
University of Southern California

LICENSING REQUIREMENT:
California – must have completed a residency in Otolaryngology-Head & Neck Surgery

APPOINTMENT LEVEL:
Clinical Fellow – Facial Plastic & Reconstructive Surgery in the Department of Otolaryngology at the University of Southern California, Keck School of Medicine

OPERATING PRIVILEGES:
Fellow will be granted privileges at Lasky Clinic and at hospitals affiliated with the University of Southern California through the Department of Otolaryngology-Head and Neck Surgery.

OPERATIVE EXPERIENCE:
Lasky Clinic offers the fellow an experience in a full range of cosmetic facial plastic surgical procedures. The fellow assists on Dr. Frankel's cases at the on-site private operating rooms. Additionally the fellow has exposure to different injection and laser skin resurfacing procedures. The fellow is the primary surgeon or the supervisory surgeon on cases through USC, and has the option to participate in trauma and reconstructive cases at USC. The fellow may have the opportunity to act as the primary surgeon on his/her private cases in the later stage of the fellowship. There is ample opportunity to observe or assist other surgeons at the Lasky Clinic or in the vicinity when time permits.

RESEARCH:
Clinical research while at Lasky Clinic. Opportunity to assist with animal, lab, or clinical research while at USC.

TEACHING RESPONSIBILITIES:
USC resident lectures will be given by the fellow regularly. The fellow will also supervise the residents in surgery. The fellow will also be responsible for organizing a facial plastics journal club combined with the USC and UCLA Departments of Otolaryngology.

CASE LOAD:
Approximately 320 cases per year at Lasky Clinic; variable at USC; potential to act as primary surgeon on fellow's own private cases as experience and skill increases.

LISA DOUGLASS

CALL RESPONSIBILITIES:
The fellow will be responsible for calls for Dr. Frankel's practice. There are no call responsibilities at USC.

BENEFITS:

*Health:	Not Provided
*Stipend:	$36,000 (Covered by Dr. Frankel) ($40,000 in 2017)
*Malpractice:	Covered by Dr. Frankel
*Tail Coverage:	Included
*Other:	

ADDITIONAL INFORMATION:
Fellowship granted time off for exams, academic meetings, and job interviews. Additionally, fellow will be given one week of paid vacation time. Vacation time will not be allowed if Dr. Frankel is away at the same time.

SURGICAL SKILLS CHECKLIST

All MSIII Surgery Students are required to be supervised performing the following skills at least three times by an attending, resident, mid-level provider or nurse specialist. Skills that are not required but are recommended were added to this list because residents from varied disciplines were surveyed and felt that practicing these skills as a third year student, regardless of chosen specialty would be helpful for future competency.

Signatures of supervisors are required. This form must be submitted to the clerkship office at the end of the clerkship.

Student Name: _____

ABDOMINAL EXAM (especially peritonitis) *must be observed by a faculty member, i.e. attending, fellow or MSE

1 Signature	2. Signature	3. Signature

VASCULAR EXAM *must be observed by a faculty member, i.e. attending, fellow or MSE

1. Signature	2. Signature	3. Signature

FOCUSED HISTORY *must be observed by a faculty member, i.e. attending, fellow or MSE

1. Signature	2. Signature	3. Signature

ABG & ALLEN'S TEST

1 Signature	2. Signature	3. Signature

CERVICAL COLLAR MANAGEMENT AND DOCUMENTATION

1. Signature	2. Signature	3. Signature

CERVICAL COLLAR REMOVAL AND DOCUMENTATION

1. Signature	2. Signature	3. Signature

IV INSERTION

1 Signature	2. Signature	3. Signature

IV REMOVAL

1. Signature	2. Signature	3. Signature

28

185

dates.

B. OSCE REMEDIATION PROCESS

The Objective Structured Clinical Examination (OSCE) is a way to assess the student's clinical skills in a standardized and summative fashion in a high-stakes setting. The OSCE score is a composite of some or all of the following performance skills: Data Gathering (History Taking and Physical Examination), Communication (Patient-Physician Interaction), and Post-Encounter Note Documentation during standardized patient encounters. The scores are not a direct translation of the proportion of actions needed to be taken but rather an overall representation of the student's competency in the management of the patient. Each clerkship has different criteria for identifying students in need of OSCE remediation based on the type of encounter, the difficulty of cases, and the

15

differential importance given to the skill domains. Once a student is identified as needing remediation, the following steps need to be taken:

- SELF-REFLECTION EXERCISE: The student must contact the Clinical Skills Education and Evaluation Center (CSEEC) to schedule an appointment to complete a SELF-REFLECTION EXERCISE based on a video review of the encounters. The CSEEC will retain the completed Self-Reflection Form and forward it to the Clerkship Director (CD) with a copy to the Medical Student Educators (MSEs) in time for the feedback session. Also, the student can check with CSEEC to determine the date and time of the repeat OSCE. (Contact: Joy Cruz at joy.cruz@med.usc.edu or 323-442-3483)

- RECEIVE FEEDBACK: The student must notify the relevant CD/MSE of the scheduled "self-reflection exercise" date by email so she/he will know when to expect the completed assignment. The CD/MSE will give feedback based on a review of performance and the self-reflection exercise results. An individualized remediation plan may be developed and a timeline for completion will be determined by the CD/MSE.
  Note: The OSCE score is only one component of the clerkship grade. OSCE remediation is intended to provide the student with the means to strengthen his/her clinical skills, and to improve performance on subsequent OSCEs, the CPX, and Step 2 CS.

IX. MEDICAL STUDENT TIME REQUIREMENTS AND DAYS OFF

Student hours include the following limits: a maximum of twenty eight hours in the hospital over one period and a maximum of 80 hours per week averaged over four weeks. Students receive at least one day off per week. Off days vary and are determined by the senior resident or attending. Holidays off are team dependent. Please see the KSOM Duty Hours Policy which can be found in the Clerkship Learning Resources.

186

NG TUBE INSERTION		
1. Signature	2. Signature	3. Signature

NG TUBE MANAGEMENT		
1. Signature	2. Signature	3. Signature

NG TUBE REMOVAL		
1. Signature	2. Signature	3. Signature

The following are not required but recommended

DIAGNOSIS OF CELLULITIS vs. NECROTIZING FASCIITIS(not required but recommended)		
1. Signature	2. Signature	3. Signature

DIAGNOSIS OF INFECTED WOUND/INCISION(not required but recommended)		
1. Signature	2. Signature	3. Signature

I & D (not required but recommended)		
1. Signature	2. Signature	3. Signature

STERILE TECHNIQUE(not required but recommended)		
1. Signature	2. Signature	3. Signature

WHEN TO CALL A SURGERY CONSULT(not required but recommended)		
1. Signature	2. Signature	3. Signature

WOUND CARE, DRSGS, PACKING, WOUND VAC (not required but recommended)		
1. Signature	2. Signature	3. Signature

As a part of the OSCE, there is an OSATS component. Students will be required to perform two of the skills found in the Skills and Thrills Manual, some of which are listed above. In addition, students will be required to answer questions on paper related to a number of the skills in the manual, including procedural steps, indications, contraindications and needed equipment.

AY2016-17

Made in the USA
Lexington, KY
29 May 2018